Six String Journal

A Technical Workout for Classical Guitar

Level 1 - Base Building

By Leonardo Garcia

Six String Journal

A Technical Workout for Classical Guitar

Level 1 - Base Building

By Leonardo Garcia

© 2016 by Six String Journal and Leonardo Garcia

BASE BUILDING

The following workout is broken down into left hand movements, right hand movements, and scales. Try to get into the habit of going through the complete workout every day or over the course of two days for several weeks at tempos slow enough where all movements are clear, controlled, and fluid. Then bit by bit, increase tempo as movements become more comfortable and reliable.

Keep a log or journal of your progress at the end of the book with reflections, note which movements are more difficult or more comfortable, and keep track of tempo. This process is all about self-discovery.

Good luck!

LEFT HAND MOVEMENTS

PART 1

Basic left hand movements – It is crucial during base building to focus on achieving clarity through accurate and efficient movements. Never sacrifice precision for speed.

Complete steps 1-3 with all the following left hand finger combinations:

Single Finger Movements: 01, 10, 02, 20, 03, 30, 04, 40
Single Pair Finger Movements: 12, 21, 23, 32, 34, 43, 13, 31, 24, 42, 14, 41

For the right hand, using *im* either free stroke or light rest stroke is fine. Using thumb *(p)* throughout is fine as well. Keep in mind the focus should be on the deliberate and precise placement of the left hand fingers. Do not complicate things with nifty right hand fingerings.

Step 1 – Perform all movements without slurs (example below using 12 and 21)

Step 2 – Perform all movements with slurs (example below using 12 and 21)

Step 3 – Build endurance by extending the time on each string (example below using 12)

Go very slowly. Listen very carefully. Do several repetitions. Explore various positions.

PART 2

Complete steps 4-6 with all the following left hand finger combinations:

Two Pair – 12 34, 43 21, 13 24, 42 31, 14 23, 32 41

Compound – 121, 212, 232, 323, 343, 434, 131, 313, 242, 424, 141, 414

Step 4 – Start all movements without slurs (example using 12 34 and 121)

Step 5 – Incorporate slurs

Step 6 – Build endurance

PART 3

Complete steps 7-9 with all the following left hand finger combinations:

Three Finger Movements – 124, 421, 134, 431, 123, 321, 234, 432
Four Finger Movements – 1234, 4321 (these two are the most important)

Step 7– Start movements without slurs (example using 124)

Step 8 – Incorporate slurs (examples using 124 and 1234)

Step 9 – Build endurance

Explore these movements in several positions.

RIGHT HAND MOVEMENTS

PART 1

This first part of this section focuses on developing the macro movement of the hand as a unit using chordal and rasgueado movements. With the exception of the rasgueado movements, begin with the right hand positioned over strings 4, 3, 2, 1 with fingers *p, i, m, a*, respectively. This is a default position to develop throughout this workout.

Step 1

Chordal Movements – *pima*, *pim* *a*, *pi* *ma*, *pma* *i*, *pm* *ia*, *pia* *m*, *pa* *im*

Groups of fingers that are underlined move together and alternate with the next finger/fingers. Below is an example of *pim a*. Since using open strings is boring, I tend to use a simple scale of thirds or a diminished 7th chord (think Villa Lobos) as I ascend and descend the fretboard. Go through all fingerings for each movement.

Step 2

Rasgueado movements – *cami, amii, pai, camii, im mi, paip*

For the movements below, rest the thumb (*p*) on string 5 or 4 when not using it in the pattern. Movement should originate from the knuckles outwards. Time to develop those flexors. Don't overdo it though!

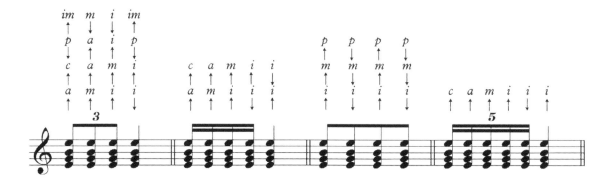

PART 2

This section begins with thumb with one other finger (*pi, pm, pa*) and proceeds to the thumb with two other finger movements (*pim, pmi, pma, pam, pia, pai*). The primary goals with the following drills are to develop a strong sense of how the fingers fall across the strings. This will reinforce our default right hand position and develop a strong sense of independence from finger to finger (i.e. the movement of one finger or stroke should not displace the hand from this default position).

Thumb with one finger movements (*pi, pm, pa*)

The fingers of the right hand not involved in the movement should passively rest by very lightly touching their respective string. If this is too difficult at first, have them float as close as possible above their respective string (*p*=4, *i*=3, *m*=2, *a*=1).

Step 1

Focus on absolute simultaneity of each pair of fingers.

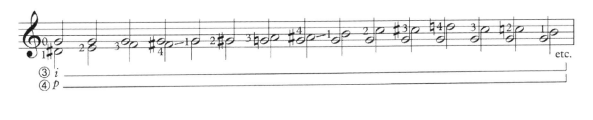

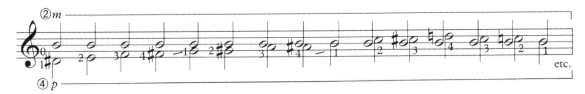

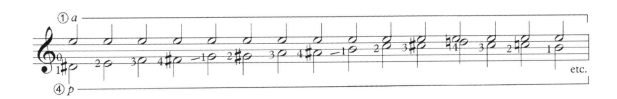

Step 2 – Proceed to alternation

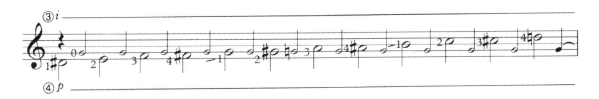

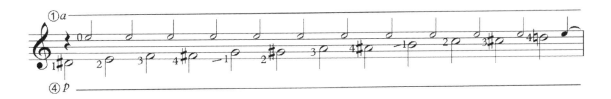

Step 3

Proceed to work on the following thumb with two finger movements (*pim, pmi, pma, pam, pia, pai*). Note that each line contains six different movements to develop.

PREPARATORY MOVEMENTS FOR SCALES

Focus on the following key points:

1) Practice perfect alternation – As the finger performing the stroke moves towards its resting point, the next finger should release from its resting point to prepare the next stroke.

2) Keep everything relaxed – The only energy used is in the stroke, once this is performed the finger should release all energy and tension. In the best case scenario, the tension of the finger is released as the alternating finger exerts energy on the next stroke.

3) If you are still developing a technical base, spend more time on the basics – *im, ma, ia* and finger alternation with *p* are the more important fingerings to develop as all the others contain these basic movements.

Spend as much time within each step or rhythm to achieve improved tone consistency, efficiency of the stroke, rhythmic precision, and perhaps, speed. Use the 2nd or 3rd string as a starting point before exploring other strings. If your nails wear easily, protect them with packing tape or keep most of your practice relegated to the first three strings. Don't forget to use a metronome!

Rest Stroke or Apoyando

Step 1

Develop rest-stroke fingerings: *im, mi, ma, am, ia, ai, p, ami, ima, imam, amim, aimi*

Step 2

Develop string-crossing: *im, mi, ma, am, ia, ai*

Step 3

Apply movements to simple coordination movements.

Perform the preparatory movements in various positions on various strings.

Free Stroke or Tirando

Step 1

Develop free-stroke fingerings: *im, mi, ma, am, ia, ai, pi, pm, pa, ami, ima, imam, amim, aimi, pmi, pami*

Step 2

Develop string crossing: *im, mi, ma, am, ia, ai, pi, pm, pa*

Step 3

Apply to simple coordination movements

Perform the preparatory movements in various positions on various strings.

SCALES

Bring It All Together

Proceed to work on the following scale forms with fingerings *im* and *ma* with both rest stroke and free stroke. There are other fingerings to develop but *im* and *ma* are inherently the most common and are found within others so before exploring those focus on the basics. Play them at numerous times each in quarter, eighth notes, triplets, and sixteenths.

Change the way in which you play through them with dynamics, extremes (very soft, very slow, very loud, very fast), and tempo. Explore left hand pressure, softness, tone balance, sound quality, legato, staccato, fingertip contact, the release, and as much detail to imprint a very clear and accurate image in your mind of what it sounds like and feels like to play well.

"The practice of scales solves the greatest number of technical problems in the shortest amount of time."

— Andrés Segovia

Basic One-Octave Scale Forms

Rest-stroke fingerings:

im, mi, ma, am, ia, ai

p, ami, ima, imam, amim, aimi

Free-stroke fingerings:

im, mi, ma, am, ia, ai, pi, pm, pa,

ami, ima, imam, amim, aimi, pmi, pami

C Major starting on string 3

C Harmonic Minor starting on string 3

C Melodic Minor starting on string 3

Basic One-Octave Scale Forms

Rest-stroke fingerings:

im, mi, ma, am, ia, ai

p, ami, ima, imam, amim, aimi

Free-stroke fingerings:

im, mi, ma, am, ia, ai, pi, pm, pa,

ami, ima, imam, amim, aimi, pmi, pami

C Major starting on string 4

C Harmonic Minor starting on string 4

C Melodic Minor starting on string 4

Basic One-Octave Scale Forms

Rest-stroke fingerings:

im, mi, ma, am, ia, ai

p, ami, ima, imam, amim, aimi

Free-stroke fingerings:

im, mi, ma, am, ia, ai, pi, pm, pa,

ami, ima, imam, amim, aimi, pmi, pami

C Major starting on string 5

C Harmonic Minor starting on string 5

C Melodic Minor starting on string 5

Basic One-Octave Scale Forms

Rest-stroke fingerings:

im, mi, ma, am, ia, ai

p, ami, ima, imam, amim, aimi

Free-stroke fingerings:

im, mi, ma, am, ia, ai, pi, pm, pa,

ami, ima, imam, amim, aimi, pmi, pami

C Chromatic starting on string 3

C Chromatic starting on string 4

C Chromatic starting on string 5

Bonus from Six String Journal:

Leo Brouwer's Axioms

Years ago, I came across an article on a Spanish site guitarra.artepulsado.com posted by Oscar López who had taken notes during a summer course with the great Cuban composer and guitarist, Leo Brouwer. The title of the post was *Axiomas básicos de Leo Brouwer*. I found the word file and thought I'd translate it for all non-Spanish speakers. It provides a wealth of advice. I've added a few commentaries below to expand the ideas a bit. Hope they are helpful.

Warm Up

Use chromatic octaves for the left hand and arpeggios and rasgueados for the right hand. Play close to the body in higher resonant positions upon starting your practice.

*I think this may mean to start your practice without having the left hand in an extended position. Starting in higher positions is less stressful for the left hand.

Speed and Scales

Use fixed, non-shifting positions in the left hand that are close to the body (i.e. higher positions) to play short bursts of notes. Play bursts in short *crescendos* (soft to loud or light to intense). Start on one string, then expand to two strings. Add one note at a time and pause between each mini-scale.

Add color and articulations to scales.

Left Hand Shifting

Left-hand notes should be played staccato (*perhaps he means before a shift). Focus on the arrival (not the departure) as you shift from 1st to 2nd, 1st to 3rd, 1st to 4th, etc., position.

Left Hand Independence

With a fixed first finger bar, play slurs and scales across all the strings with the rest of the fingers. Try all combinations possible.

Memory

To avoid embedding errors, do not start memorizing at the very beginning of learning a piece.

Fingerings

There are never definitive fingerings.

*What Brouwer most likely means to covey here is that fingerings evolve throughout the lifetime of learning a piece. Inevitably, we discover better, more efficient, more musical, more interesting ways to play passages and discard or change older fingerings as our familiarity with the piece increases.

Color

Exploit the three primary sonorous zones of the guitar: over the sound hole (resonant zone), over right part of the rosette (resonant and clarity zone), and near the bridge (clarity zone).

Harmonics

Do not pluck harmonics diagonally.

PRACTICE JOURNAL

Week 1	Notes

Week 2	Notes

Week 3	Notes

Week 4	Notes

Leonardo Garcia
Classical Guitarist

Described as "a faithful interpreter of Mangore's musical art" by Alirio Diaz and as "conscientious, intelligent, musical, and technically impeccable" by Eliot Fisk, Leo Garcia is an award-winning classical guitarist, recording artist, author, and sought-after educator.

As a performer, Garcia has performed across North America, South America, and Europe, as both a soloist and as a chamber musician. As an educator, he has worked with hundreds of children and families for over 15 years through KinderGuitar. His writings have appeared in *Guitar Review*, the popular KinderGuitar blog (kinderguitar.com), and Six String Journal (sixstringjournal.com), and he has acted as jury member, performer, and lecturer at musical festivals such as the Bay Area's Junior Bach Festival, the Boston Guitar Festival, the Yale Guitar Extravaganza, and the Guitar Foundation of America's International Festival.

Leo grew up in Venezuela but left to pursue higher education in the U.S., eventually earning a B.A. in economics from Yale, an M.M. and Artist Diploma from the Yale School of Music, and a Graduate Performance degree from the New England Conservatory, before founding and developing the KinderGuitar music education system. The success of KinderGuitar led quickly to its expansion, and now with three San Francisco Bay Area locations and one in New Mexico, KinderGuitar offers training and licensing to highly qualified aspiring educators to help them create successful and sustainable music-teaching studios for children in their communities.

www.sixstringjournal.com

Printed in Great Britain
by Amazon